ONION BASED

P.E.E.L

The steps to building, retaining, and expanding relationships

John H. Brown

All Rights Reserved
Copyright © 2023 by John H. Brown
No part of this book may be reproduced or transmitted, downloaded, distributed, reverse engineered, or stored in or introduced into any information storage and retrieval system, in any form or by any means, including photocopying and recording, whether electronic or mechanical, now known or hereinafter invented without permission in writing from the author.
Author: John H. Brown
Brown Developments, Inc.
Visit our website at *www.browndevelopments.com*

Table of Contents

Glossary of Abbreviations and Acronyms

3Ds of Success: Define-Develop-Deliver	3Ds
Account Management Lifecycle	AML
Account Management Team	AMT
Account Manager	AM
Account Review Process	ARP
Account Transition Form	ATF
Acknowledge-Confirm-Execute	ACE
Annual Strategy Meeting	ASM
Customer-Based Marketing	CBM
Customer Success Manager	CSM
Initial Sales Team	IST
Monthly Meeting	MM
Objectives-Priorities-Initiatives	OPI
People-Energy-Emotion-Leading	PEEL
Product Team	PT
Product Marketing Team	PMT

☐	Quarterly Business Review	QBR
☐	Return on Investment	ROI
☐	Sales Engineer	SE
☐	Service Level Agreement	SLA
☐	Solutions Specialist	SS

Introduction

I will start out by thanking you for picking up a copy of Onion Based-Relationships. I have learned throughout my 50-plus years of life the value of gratitude, and the power of thank you. My desire is always to share experiences that have positively impacted my life and others. I am blessed to be surrounded by good people who I allow to help guide my thought process. This level of association, my drive, belief in self, and the Universe have enabled me to appreciate life at a high level. If you can utilize some of my personal experiences to achieve your goals, then I have fulfilled my purpose. So here I am with another building block to the Onion Based concept. Onion Based-Relationships provide a simple process that can be duplicated when applicable. I call it a building block because I am picking up where Onion Based-Selling left off.

The PEEL Method, introduced in Onion Based-Selling, applies here and any time I/you are dealing with people. There are always *People* with a certain level of *Energy* and *Emotion* depending on what they are dealing with. The same people have a need or desire to *Lead or be led* through challenges and blind spots to achieve whatever they deem is a success. You do not have to, but it will help if you read Onion Based-Selling first.

Account Management Lifecycle

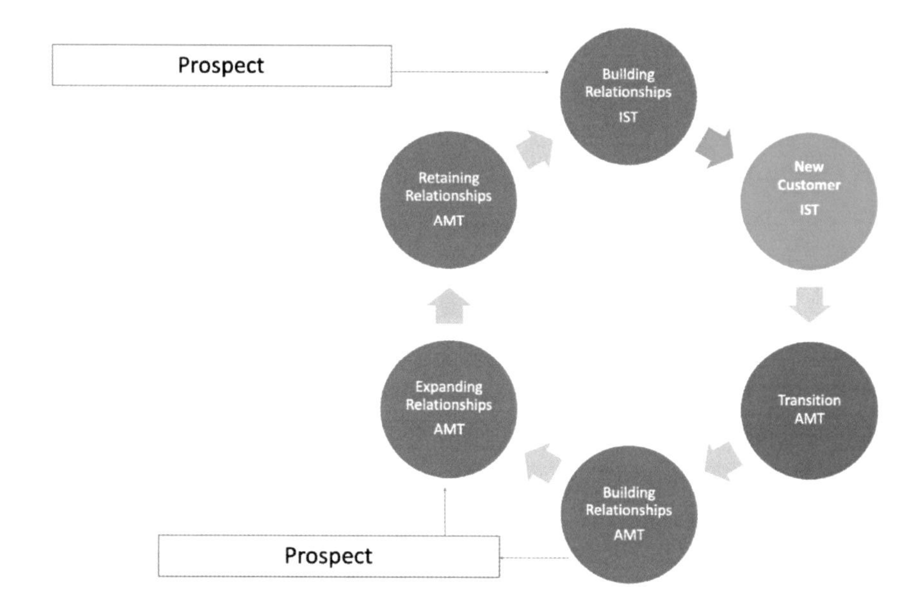

The first book, Onion Based-Selling, has a Net-New Logo Hunter focus. It walks you through the initial phase of meeting a prospect, building rapport, earning trust, and winning their business. Onion Based-Relationships, is the second book in the series that focuses on account management. I share the process when those customers are transitioned from the Initial Sales team (IST) to the Account Management team (AMT). I will break down how to continue building upon those relationships and what needs to be done to expand and retain them. It is less expensive to keep a customer than to find a new one. Keeping a customer is about consistently communicating with them, checking the boxes to their needs, and delivering value. There has always been the need to do so, but it is even more important when economic conditions become uncertain, budgets tighten and dry up. If you do not have a way of measuring value, showing how to drive growth, and creating a significant impact, you have a strong chance of losing what you have worked so hard for. You must prove it or lose it.

As we all know, life does not provide a victory at every opportunity. There will be losses. Most of them can be traced back to poor communication and execution. Although frustrating, the better we become at learning the lessons, the greater our chances of winning and being catapulted to significant levels of success. I personally hate losing. I tell myself it is my practice ground. It keeps me in a state of growing with a desire to learn more and become better. I leverage the lessons, take counsel from my trusted advisors, and come back with a better plan to execute.

One of the keys to success in all areas of life and in sales is consistent communication. Authentic conversations allow you to have the more challenging ones when they come up. The better the communication, with the desire to understand and adjust when needed, creates a path to:

- Building Relationships
- Expanding Relationships
- Retaining Relationships

As of June 2023, I can happily say I have been with my wife, Jacqueline, for 28 years and married 26 of them. We still date each other. It keeps the spice in life. Most of our time is centered around conversation. We have fun with it and name some of the conversations. Friday evening is Cocktails & Conversation, and Saturday and Sunday mornings are Coffee & Conversation. They also happen during power walks and working out together. We are always having conversations.

The conversations are geared toward what good things are happening when we are apart, what challenges we are working through, asking each other for advice, and/or just listening. Over the years, we have both evolved in several areas. Our communication includes vulnerability, trust, and respect. It is vital to us becoming the best version of ourselves as individuals and as a couple.

Define + Develop + Deliver
3Ds of Success®

Jacqueline and I never claim to know it all or be perfect. We are students of life with an ongoing desire to learn and grow. We are consistent readers as well as content creators. If something works, we waste no time applying it in our lives. We seek, identify, and leverage tools and resources that help us stay on track and advance. In 2020, I created a simple framework called 3Ds of Success (3Ds). We pride ourselves on *drinking our own champaign*. If you are not familiar with that term, it means we use the same tools we create because we believe in them. The 3Ds of Success are Define + Develop + Deliver. No matter what is going on, we are constantly *Defining* where we are and what we want to accomplish, collaborating to *Develop* a plan/strategy, and working together to *Deliver*/execute our desired results in a timely manner. We both take this attitude into our business lives. For me, it is in sales. I have found the more connected I am to my customers as people, the more successful the relationships are. They are going through things just like I am, so the better we communicate with each other, the more successful the relationships are.

Onion Based-Relationships is written from the Account Management perspective. Not every company views Account Management the same. Some have the Account Manager (AM) and Customer Success Manager (CSM) engage the customer separately. It is more of an individual engagement approach where the AMs are solely responsible for sales and expansion via upselling and cross-selling. They leave adoption, service, and retention to the CSM, and the AM comes in for Quarterly Business Reviews (QBRs) and to assist the CSM in renewing the business. I feel this type of relationship is riskier because both the AM and CSM may not be as in tune with each other or the customer. This model can create blind spots on what is holistically happening with the account. I will share what I feel is the perfect relationship between the AM, CSM, SS, and Internal Partners when working with customers for overall account success.

Account Management Team & Internal Partners

Core Roles:

Account Manager (AM): The role is crucial in building, expanding, and retaining successful relationships with customers and contributing to the growth of a company. This is done by understanding customer needs, how they map to products/services that align with the customer's goals, and partnering with the Customer Success Manager (CSM) and Solutions Specialist (SS) on account strategies and action plans. In addition, resolving issues where needed, identify upsell and cross-sell opportunities, achieve/exceed sales targets, handle negotiations and contract renewals, and collaborate with the SS and CSM to avoid blind spots and enhance the customer experience.

Customer Success Manager (CSM): The role of the CSM is like the AM when it comes to understanding customer needs and how they map to products/services that align with the customer's goals.

Partnering with the AM on account strategies and action plans and partnering with Customer Support (CS) as a liaison between them and the customer when product issues occur. In addition, they are involved in helping maximize adoption and engagement, working to turn satisfied customers into advocates for the company, and collaborating with the SS and AM to avoid blind spots and enhance the customer experience.

Solutions Specialist (SS) or Sales Engineer (SE): A solutions specialist is a professional who is responsible for helping customers identify and implement solutions to their problems. They work closely with the AM, CSM, and customers to understand challenges and needs. They use this information to develop customized solutions leveraging company products/services to solve challenges and meet customer needs.

When AM, CSM, and SS work together, the partnership benefits both the company and the customer. By working together, they reduce the time it takes to understand customer needs and how to meet them. The SS can provide insights into the why and how to maximize the company's products/services. This positions the AM to propose solutions and pricing that align with immediate and sometimes long-term needs. It also enables the CSM to better engage with the customer on adoption. This level of collaboration shows a unified team that is focused on helping its customers achieve their Objectives, Priorities, and Initiatives (OPIs) in a timely manner.

Internal Partners:

Sales & Customer Success Leadership: Leadership plays a critical role in ensuring that AMT is focused, motivated, and capable of effectively managing accounts to drive growth and revenue for the company and its customers. Their support ensures the AMT has the resources and tools necessary to effectively manage accounts. They must also provide guidance on complex issues, coaching to improve performance, and help where needed so the team achieves its targets.

Product Team (PT): Ultimately, all our success is dependent on the product doing what it is marketed to do and reliably. The customer feedback loop to the product team is crucial. It is often overlooked as the Development team(s) are generally overwhelmed and building new features to close new deals. Meanwhile, the existing customers struggle with existing functionality that is not there or not user-friendly. This is a relationship that is critical to 'get stuff done' for your customers.

Product Marketing Team (PMT): Product Marketing ensures the right product is developed for the right audience and that it is successfully brought to market in a way that resonates with customers and drives business growth. It requires a deep understanding of the product, the market, and the target customers, as well as strong communication and analytical skills.

Customer-Based Marketing (CBM): The role of a Customer-Based Marketing specialist is to develop and implement a customer-centric marketing strategy for a company. This involves gathering and analyzing customer data, creating customer personas, developing personalized messaging, creating marketing materials that appeal to specific customer segments, and measuring and analyzing the effectiveness of marketing campaigns. This approach seeks to build long-term relationships with customers by providing them with personalized experiences, offers, and content at the best time. The more engaged this team is with the AMT, the better. The AMT can provide real-time updates on the health of the account so marketing can deliver content at optimal times.

Customer Support: These Agents/Representatives are responsible for ensuring that customers have a positive experience with their company's products/services. Their primary purpose is to assist customers with questions, concerns, or challenges they may be having with the products/services and to provide resolution in a timely and satisfactory manner according to Service Level Agreements (SLAs). The also partner with the CSM and sometimes the AM to ensure the communication to the customer during challenges is timely as they resolve and implement solutions.

Order Management & Billing Specialist: The role of an Order Management and Billing Specialist is to ensure that customer orders are processed accurately, efficiently, and billed correctly, and work with the AMT and customer on any discrepancies.

Finance Specialist: A team to analyze market data, assess cost structures, and develop pricing models. When working with the AM, they provide financial guidance and support to ensure that deals are financially sound and aligned with the organization's strategic goals to optimize pricing while remaining competitive.

Contracts & Legal: When working with the AM, a contracts and legal specialist plays a critical role in ensuring that sales deals are legally sound and the organization's interests are protected. This can involve reviewing the terms and conditions of the contract, identifying potential legal risks, protecting intellectual property, providing guidance to the sales team on how to mitigate those risks, and potentially resolving legal disputes.

The significance of me pointing out the core and internal roles is to show all the people it takes to build, expand, and retain customer relationships. Customer-Centric companies that have a *delighting the customer* culture tend to have strong internal collaboration between the various departments. This level of teamwork creates a sense of shared responsibility and accountability and ultimately leads to an improved overall customer experience.

Net New Customer:

Some call the initial sale "land." It typically refers to making a successful sale/closing a deal, thereby converting a prospect to an actual paying customer/Net New. After a period, the customer is transitioned to the AMT to "expand" and retain. The expansion opportunity is centered around the customer experience. If the product/service in tandem with IST has delivered on expectations, the AMT is set up for success. If not, there will be steps to take to earn back trust and move forward.

At some point in the first year, new customers are transitioned to the AMT. That transition moves everyone to the next step in the Account Management Lifecycle. I call it passing the baton.

I am excited to peel back more layers with you. Onion Based-Relationships is my *perfect world perspective* of account management. I will blend in personal experiences, challenges faced, and actions we took that led to better communication, results needed to drive the business forward, and, most of all, *delighting the customer.*

Now let's get into it.

Chapter 1: Passing the Baton

Account Management Lifecycle

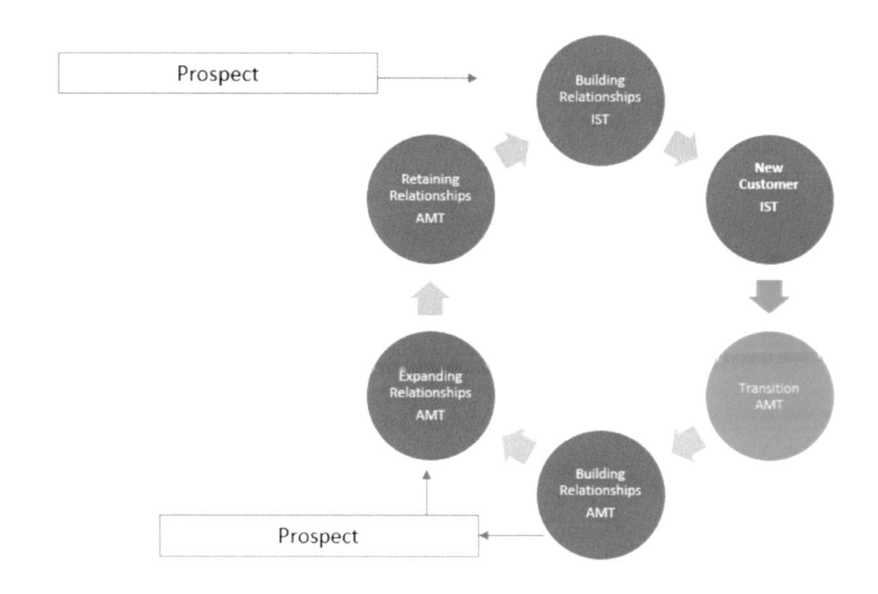

Passing the Baton

As we move forward, imagine yourself being the salesperson/AM or one of the core or internal partner roles. I will use 3Ds as the framework to keep you on track while you navigate the Account Management Lifecycle (AML). The better you know what phase you are at in the journey, the more layers you will be able to peel back, and the more success you will have. There are two impression points with a significant impact on a customer relationship. They are:

- The Initial Sale
- The Transition

The Initial Sale is done by the New Logo Hunter/Initial Sales Team (IST). They take the prospect through a sales process to understand who they are, their business, its objectives, priorities, initiatives, challenges to overcome, timeframe to resolve, budget, and decision-makers. The IST leverages this data to qualify if Objectives, Priorities, Initiatives (OPIs), and challenges align with their company's products/services offering. If so, they move forward to proposal, negotiation, procurement, and, when all goes well, onboarding. The ideal relationship will have the IST outline the customer journey. In that conversation, the IST can speak to and show the customer the various internal teams they will work with, the role they play, review the transition process to the Account Management Team (AMT), and the role they play in the long-term relationship. This process prepares the customer for the long-term relationship and shows them your sales teams know what they are doing and how your organization values the overall customer experience.

Once a customer has been with your company for 6-months months or more, they know where your product/service and company excel, as well as the shortcomings. The IST and internal partner's ability to meet and exceed customer expectations in the first year of the contract creates the foundation for a long-term relationship.

Significant questions: Is the product/service working as promised? If not, is the customer being heard and challenges resolved in a timely manner by the appropriate teams? In addition, how engaged is the IST that sold the deal? If they have a one-and-done mindset, the transition will be in jeopardy. The term "Delighting the Customer" should always be the focus. Take care of them, and they will take care of you by staying.

Delighting the Customer is not hard. Use the A.C.E. concept to increase your percentage of success. Your actions should always show the customer how important they are. They will know because, during every conversation, you will *Acknowledge* what they are telling you, *Confirm* what they have told you so they know you are listening, and then *Execute* what you said you would do. If there are challenges, everyone needed for resolution is focused and ready to support the steps outlined in a clearly defined Action Plan. Gaining buy-in for anything you are collaborating on is very important. I call it getting to "We." When all parties mutually agree on the plan and collectively move forward to execute it.

The Transition from the IST to the AMT is crucial. It is like passing the baton in a relay race. If you do not execute the handoff, you risk dropping the baton, and the race/relationship is in jeopardy. That is why I believe in a formal handoff process. It begins with the IST completing the Account Transition Form (ATF), reviewing it with the AMT, and then facilitating a warm handoff meeting introducing the AMT to the customer. The ATF has all the data required for the AMT to have a clear picture of who the customer is. When the AMT and the customer know what they are both walking into, it leads to a smooth transition. It is a two-step process.

Step 1: IST to AMT: This is an internal meeting where both teams come together to review the ATF and address questions and any concerns in the current relationship. The ATF includes some of the following data: Why did the customer buy? Is your company delivering to the customer's expectations? Who are the key players? Who are the blockers? What is the structure of the organization? What is going well? What is not going well? How can your company improve? What should the AMT continue doing to keep the relationship strong and build upon it? What is the contractual situation? What is the customer's procurement process? Is the IST able to facilitate a warm handoff so the baton is passed and not dropped? The ATF becomes the tool that can be easily shared, making the transition as seamless as possible.

Step 2: Customer Introduction Meeting: This is where the IST introduces the customer to the AMT. During this warm handoff, the AMT can confirm what they know. The AMT can use this time to level set with the customer. *Define* their mindset: Why did they buy? Do they feel their expectations are being met? What is going well? What is not going well? What can be improved? What should the AMT continue doing to keep the relationship strong and build upon it? What is their understanding of the contractual situation and procurement process? If given the opportunity to renew at that moment, would they? Whatever they say, the AMT should be ready to enter the *Develop* a Plan stage. This stage is where the AMT creates an Action Plan to right the ship in an agreed-upon timeframe if the customer is not happy. If they are happy, it will be documenting the steps to continue moving forward, helping them achieve their OPIs. When you *Deliver* what you say you will do, you are "Delighting the customer."

Positioning for Consistency: I am a firm believer in setting expectations upfront. It may not happen this way, but in a perfect world, during the *Define* stage, the AMT outlines a regular meeting cadence, and the customer agrees to it. This cadence becomes part of the plan in the *development* stage. When the AMT meets with the customer, they can check the boxes on execution. The purpose is to ensure value is being *delivered* and can be measured to show progress against their OPIs.

Customer Engagement: I was taught years ago never to leave a meeting without booking the next one. This sets the expectation there is a follow-up conversation to peel back more layers and go deeper. The purpose is to keep the customer engaged. Most are familiar with Quarterly Business Reviews (QBRs). If executed in partnership with your customers and key internal partners, they can be very productive. During the Transition meeting, gain buy-in with the customer. Let them know the best practice is to have at least four benchmark meetings per year and smaller monthly meetings.

During these meetings, the AMT will ask questions and listen to assess, acknowledge, and adjust the Action Plan. It also ensures everyone is in alignment and moving forward with the same plan. Here is a framework I feel works well. Call it a Kickoff meeting if it follows the Transition meeting. Post the Transition meeting, use the same format each year, but call it an Annual Strategy Meeting (ASM). Back this meeting up with a QBR, and between QBRs, have Monthly Meetings (MMs) whenever possible. This may not line up perfectly with your customers if they operate on a fiscal calendar or if their budget is not aligned with this format but use this as a guide and adjust according to what works best for your customers.

- January: Annual Kickoff Meeting/Annual Strategy Meeting
- February – March: Monthly Meetings
- April: Quarterly Business Review
- May – June: Monthly Meetings
- July: Quarterly Business Review
- August – September: Monthly Meetings
- October: Quarterly Business Review
- November – December: Monthly Meetings

See Diagrams:

- Account Review Process
- Monthly Meeting & Quarterly Business Review Framework

Annual Strategy Meeting (ASM): This is a one-hour collaborative meeting led by the AM, supported by the CSM, SS, and needed internal partners. The purpose is to gather C-Level executives and key stakeholders within an organization to review the previous year's performance, *define* the current state of the business, and set strategic objectives, priorities, and initiatives (OPIs) for the upcoming year. The meeting serves as a platform for aligning the entire organization around a common vision, discussing challenges and opportunities, then *developing* actionable plans and beginning to deliver on them.

Attendees:

- Customer: Executive Leadership, Key Stakeholders, Decision Makers

- Your Company: AM, CSM, SS, or any internal partners that can add value.

Quarterly Business Review (QBR): This is a one-hour collaborative meeting led by the AM, supported by the CSM, SS, and needed internal partners. The purpose is to assess the progress, performance, and key metrics of a business over a specific quarter. Unlike the ASM, which focuses on long-term goals and strategic planning, the QBR is a shorter-term evaluation that allows the AMT and customer to assess performance to date, acknowledge what is or is not working, and make the necessary adjustments to the Action Plan per quarter to ensure execution and alignment of the OPIs. This is a reminder to use each interaction to peel back more layers and build personal relationships.

Attendees:

- Customer: Key Stakeholders & Decision Makers

- Your Company: AM, CSM, SS, or any internal partners that can add value.

Monthly Meeting (MM): This is a 30-minute check-in meeting led by the CSM and supported by the AM if needed. Use it to peel back more layers, continue to build personal relationships, address concerns between QBRs, and for the CSM to provide feature/function training where needed to keep adoption and engagement high. Use the same business review framework to *assess* performance to date, *acknowledge* what is or is not working, and discuss *adjustments* to be shared with the AM and SS for the Action Plan. Everything is designed to ensure alignment with OPIs.

Attendees:

- Customer: Key Stakeholders
- Your Company: CSM and AM & internal partners if needed

See Diagrams:

- Account Review Process
- Monthly Meeting & Quarterly Business Review Framework

Account Review Process

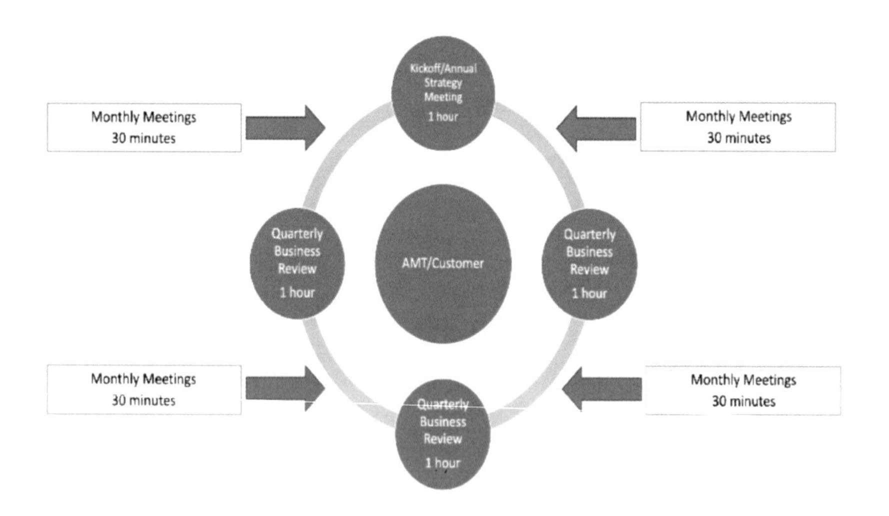

Monthly Meeting & Quarterly Business Review Framework

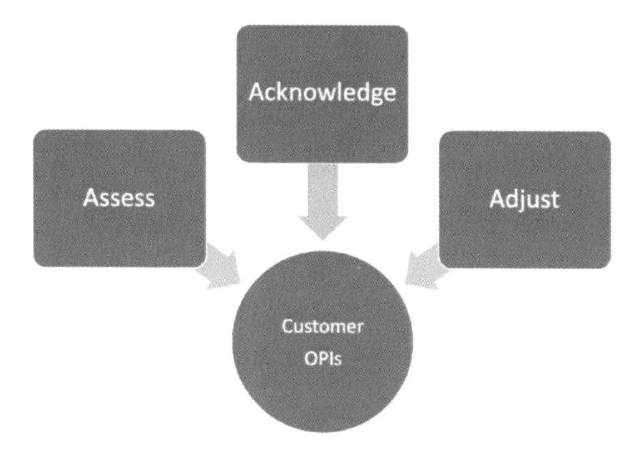

Assess: The AMT evaluates the progress on the mutually agreed upon Action Plan they have established with the customer. They do so by asking questions to gather relevant information, data, and feedback to understand what is happening and why it is happening.

Acknowledge: Once they have a clear understanding of the situation, they acknowledge the facts, feelings, and perspectives of everyone involved. This involves active listening, empathy, and communication to ensure that everyone is heard and understood.

Adjust: The final step is for them to adjust/make changes to the Action Plan as needed to improve the situation and to keep the customer on track or get them back on track with their OPIs. Use the QBR for significant adjustments.

Good vs Bad

Good: No one likes chaos and confusion. That is why I believe in a formal handoff process. It begins with the IST completing the Account Transition Form (ATF), reviewing it with the AMT, and then facilitating a warm handoff meeting introducing the AMT to the customer. When the AMT and the customer know what they are both walking into, it leads to a smooth transition. At that point, the AMT can focus on building rapport and level setting by confirming vs. asking things the customer feels should have been shared by the IST.

Bad: If the AMT is not up to speed on what is happening with the customer, it can be disastrous. The possibility of walking into immediate challenges and frustrated customers can arise if there is poor communication between the IST and the AMT. This lack of communication and proper handoff will create additional frustration for the customer, and the new relationship will be off to a bad start.

Personal Experience:

I have experienced both good and bad account transitions. I recall having a high-profile account transitioned to my AMT that was in the final year of a 2-year contract. It came with a lot of exposure due to the size of the contract and expansion potential.

Challenge: This was a bad transition moment. The ATF was 50% complete. It was missing key players, blockers, why the customer bought, and details about some missed deliverables. The Influential Seat Holder was not happy due to some missed deliverables that were tied to their company's overall objectives. Our deliverables had been pushed back on the roadmap. At no fault of the Influential Seat Holder, they looked bad to their leadership team because it was part of their business priorities to execute in the upcoming quarter. The relationship was at risk of being renewed if we did not meet their expectations in a short period of time. Fortunately, there was a warm handoff meeting with the customer because we did not have time to waste.

Actions Taken: Our AMT focused on level setting with the Influential Seat Holder. Our first step was to have a meeting to *Define* Why they bought, get clarity on the missing deliverables, and the measurable impact it was having on their business. In addition, we needed to fill in the gaps from the ATF that would help us as we navigated through the process.

We became vulnerable by empathizing with the customer and explaining that our success was directly tied to theirs. We emphasized the AMT would do everything we could to meet and exceed their expectations, no matter what their previous experience had been. They appreciated our sincerity. As the leader/AM, I began to map out what they told us in the *Define* stage and the steps it would take internally for us to provide the deliverables. I documented it and moved to *Develop*/create a plan with the CSM and the Product team/Internal Partner in charge of our roadmap. We had several internal strategy meetings to ensure we checked all the boxes and could execute the plan in the time the customer needed before we positioned it to the Influential Seat Holder.

Our AMT met with the Influential Seat Holder and their leadership team. We had to help them rebuild trust with their leaders. I brought in leadership within our company for peer-to-peer conversations. Our AMT presented the plan. The goal was to have them confirm we heard and accounted for everything they asked for. Our success would be based on them buying in, too. We were all happy when they agreed to the plan. Both sides came together and achieved "We." The AMT and internal teams jumped into the *delivery* phase. Our collective ability to execute meant the customer would be validated for the initial reasons they bought, our company would help them achieve their priorities, which fed into their business objectives, and our team/company would retain the business. The AMT and internal partners turned a bad situation into a good one.

Passing the Baton Summary: 3 Things – 3 Steps

3 Things:

1. Account Transition Form (ATF)
2. Formal account transition: Internal, then external with the customer.
3. PEEL, 3Ds of Success, Cadence.

3 Steps:

1. The IST completing the ATF is key to success. It is the blueprint for the AMT. Without details, there will be blind spots that lead to chaos and confusion.
2. The IST should coordinate a Transition meeting with the AMT. They have a relationship and rapport. Be it good or bad, they are the catalyst to make the transition to the AMT seamless and a pleasurable experience for the customer.
3. Remember, you are dealing with people. Use the PEEL method to meet them where they are. The AMT's ability to *Define* where they are in the relationship by level setting is the beginning of a new relationship. No matter what the situation is, if it is bad, they are the superheroes that have the skillset and connections to *Develop* a plan and *Deliver* upon it to right the ship. If good, they have the skillset and connections to use the 3Ds of Success (3Ds) to build upon the relationship and make it stronger. And do not forget to establish a cadence. This form of consistent communication helps to ensure you are on track with achieving OPIs.

Chapter 2: Building Relationships

Account Management Lifecycle

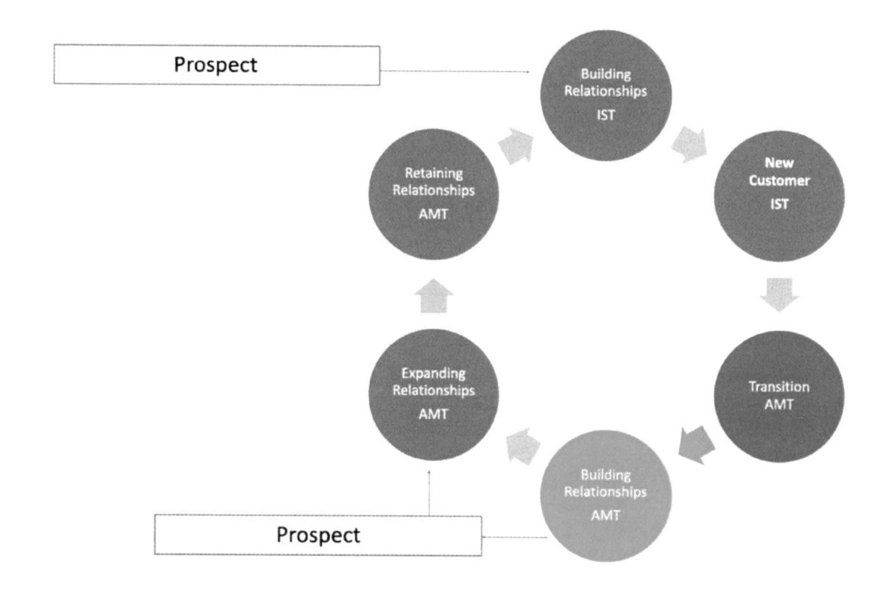

Success begins with building relationships. You will find the PEEL method to be very useful. It will help you focus on PEOPLE, channel your ENERGY to have a positive impact on their EMOTIONS, and help LEAD them to a desired goal.

Remember, the people you are selling to are more than a role in the company. They are just like you. They want to be understood, respected, and valued. Your job is to develop TRUST and create VALUE through TEAMWORK. These three areas will peel back the layers needed for significant impact.

Trust is a major component of any successful relationship. It can be built via honesty and transparency. People appreciate knowing what your agenda is. Over time, it can be built by consistently meeting deadlines, delivering on your promises, and being reliable. As previously stated, one of the success keys to the 28 years I have shared with my wife is our consistent level of communication and doing what we say we will do. It is the same with your customers.

Regular communication increases understanding and reduces chaos and confusion. Building trust takes time, effort, and commitment. The more trust you build, the more layers you peel back, and the deeper the relationship.

According to Jim Burke, former chairman and CEO of Johnson & Johnson, "You can't have success without trust. The word trust embodies almost everything you can strive for that will help you to succeed" (Covey, 2006). This key factor must be mutual between all organizations involved, whether they are suppliers of materials or providers of outsourcing capabilities. If mutual trust is established early on, all organizations will benefit through a greater willingness to share ideas and goals and work together to solve problems.

Regaining Trust: It is inevitable at some point, you will make a mistake and lose some level of trust. Once you realize you have made one, own up to it early, and communicate to your customer what happened and the steps you will take in the future to ensure it does not happen again. This allows you to repair whatever was damaged as a result of the mistake.

Value is perceived based on the results being delivered to your customer. Their personal experience is all that matters. Understand it, know it, and deliver it. This will be an ongoing process and should never end. The *Define* stage is all about uncovering the benefit the customer receives from your product/services in relation to the price they pay for it. Once this has been uncovered, continuously work to gain insights into their preferences, pain points, and desires. Then, focus your efforts on *developing* and *delivering* products/services that meet and exceed their needs and expectations. Stay connected by providing a personalized experience. Be vulnerable by sharing more about yourself so they will do the same. The more connected you are, the stronger your relationship. Then, continue to improve and overdeliver. Value shows up in 3 ways:

- Perceived: It is not solely based on the objective characteristics or features of a product/service. It is influenced by the individual's personal preferences, needs, expectations, and past experiences. When the customer can point out the benefits, advantages, and satisfaction they expect to receive from using a particular offering, then the product, sales, and marketing teams have done their job.

- Quantifiable: Provides a more objective and measurable approach to assessing the impact and effectiveness of a product/service. It enables businesses to make informed decisions, prioritize investments, justify expenditures, and communicate the value proposition to stakeholders. There are situations where return on investment (ROI) and cost savings are not easily captured to show value. In these situations, lean into perceived value because it includes subjective factors like customer satisfaction, brand reputation, and emotional appeal, which play into shaping customer behavior and decision-making.

- Achieved: It is assessed by comparing the actual outcomes with the desired or intended outcomes. It involves evaluating the extent to which the desired goals/expectations have been met or exceeded. This assessment can be based on various metrics or indicators, depending on the specific context and goals of the offering. Achieved value may not always match the initial expectations. There can be external factors, market conditions, and unforeseen circumstances that influence the realized outcomes. This is why consistent communication, evaluation, and teamwork are crucial to understand and adjust to achieve value over time.

My purpose in pointing out the 3 types of value is so you find yourself coming back to how things really are from the customer's view. According to a study by PWC, 86% of buyers are willing to pay more for a great customer experience. Additionally, at least 80% of Business-2- Business customers expect a Business-2-Business experience that is as good or better than Business-2-Consumer, demonstrating the high expectations that customers have for their business interactions. -Article written in Feb 2023.

You may believe you are delivering value based on what your Product Marketing and Sales Enablement leaders have said, but if your customer does not see it the way you do, then you are not on track and need to get back to the 3Ds.

Teamwork: Nothing big is accomplished on your own. Teamwork promotes synergy and harnesses the collective power of individuals to achieve common goals. It cultivates cooperation, fosters a positive work environment, and drives success in various endeavors. The value of teamwork is significant in various aspects of life, whether it is in the workplace, sports, or personal relationships. Here are some key reasons why teamwork is highly valued:

- Increased productivity: When individuals work together as a team, they can combine their skills, knowledge, and expertise to accomplish tasks more efficiently. Each team member can contribute their unique strengths and talents, leading to improved productivity and the ability to tackle complex challenges.

- Diverse perspectives: Teams comprised of individuals with diverse backgrounds, experiences, and viewpoints can bring fresh perspectives to problem-solving. This diversity allows for a broader range of ideas and innovative solutions that may not have been possible with a single individual working alone.

- Improved decision-making: Teams can engage in discussions and debates, considering various viewpoints and analyzing different options before making decisions. This collaborative decision-making process often leads to more informed and balanced choices, minimizing individual biases and enhancing the quality of decisions.

- Mutual support and learning: Working as a team fosters an environment of mutual support, where team members can aid, share knowledge, and learn from each other. This collective learning process can enhance individual skills, promote personal growth, and create a sense of camaraderie within the team.

- Enhanced creativity and innovation: Teamwork encourages brainstorming, idea-sharing, and out-of-the-box thinking. Collaborative environments stimulate creativity and innovation as individuals build upon each other's ideas, challenge assumptions, and generate new concepts that may not have arisen individually.

- Increased motivation and morale: Being part of a team can boost motivation and morale, as individuals feel a sense of belonging and purpose. Team members can provide encouragement, celebrate successes together, and support each other during challenging times, fostering a positive and supportive work atmosphere.

- Division of labor and specialization: Teamwork allows for the division of labor based on individual strengths and expertise. By leveraging the unique skills of each team member, tasks can be allocated efficiently, leading to a more streamlined workflow and better overall outcomes.

- Adaptability and resilience: Teams are often better equipped to handle unexpected changes, setbacks, or crises compared to individuals working alone. With shared responsibility and a collaborative mindset, teams can adapt quickly, support each other through challenges, and find creative solutions to overcome obstacles.

A successful customer relationship is when the AMT and the customer are working together with the internal teams in all areas required to deliver on their OPIs. In addition, when enough trust is built, the customer is comfortable to openly share the challenges, the results needed, and the timeframe in which to deliver them. This level of teamwork leads to delighting the customer and a high valued experience for them.

Good vs. Bad:

Good: The AMT will spend the bulk of the time with customers. Good is when: 1) The relationship is centered around the customer journey and experience. 2) The AM and the CSM have consistent engagement with each user/seat holder that has access to the products/services. 3) The customer openly shares their priorities, initiatives, and the challenges they face; it gives the AMT the opportunity to identify resources and tools that help them achieve quantifiable goals. 4) While the customer is focused on checking the boxes to achieve the overall vision, the AMT should be focused on saving them time by connecting them to key resources and tools they may not be aware of and helping reduce blind spots so they are able to move the needle forward.

This type of teamwork shows value and can be spotlighted during any business review. The more knowledge the AMT has about the individual, their role, what needs to be done, and how that role fits into the success of the organization, the better prepared they will be to provide insight and coaching to maximize the products/services the customer is paying for. The AMT's ability to deliver ongoing solutions builds trust, enhances usage, and increases the opportunity for expansion and retention.

Personal Experience:

Bad: When the seat holder is not willing to engage with the AMT. It is the feeling/question of why they purchase. Are they getting value from having access to the products/services or not? No one likes silence. The assumption from silence means the customer is not happy and will eventually churn/leave.

Changing roles is something we all will deal with. People changing roles can be beneficial for both the employee and the organization. Some common reasons for change are career growth, personal growth, business needs, organizational restructuring, and retention. Not long ago, my AMT had lunch with a Vice President (VP) in an account we had been managing for about a year. With 12 months remaining in the contract, we felt the overall relationship was going well. The AMT had a regular meeting cadence with all users/seat holders in the account, where we revisited previous, current, and future priorities. We used the Account Review Framework: Assess, Acknowledge, and Adjust in each meeting.

The VP was a champion who always spoke highly of our products/services and the way our team worked with their users. Everyone was happy. That day, the VP informed us she would be leaving the company for an amazing opportunity. Naturally, we were all sad she was leaving but happy for her continued success. We wished her well. Before leaving lunch, we asked for a warm handoff to her successor if she perceived any major changes in the overall business relationship and guidance on making it a smooth transition.

Challenge: The potential challenge was the VP leaving without the transition. That would put our team at a disposition not knowing the new leader and if they would know the level of positive impact we had been providing to the VP's team and organization overall. This happens when leaders change. They typically want to bring in their own teams and vendors from previous relationships, which causes the established vendor the need to immediately prove their value to retain the relationship. If the existing AMT cannot do so, it can lead to churn/lost business. With 12 months left in their contract, we did not want to skip a beat. Fortunately, this was not the case. The VP had already been raving about the way our AMT had been delivering on all commitments, which led to tremendous respect and trust throughout the organization.

Actions Taken: Although we had the vote of confidence and seal of approval from the transitioning VP, we had her set up a meeting with her successor. After introductions, our AMT spent most of the time showing why the organization trusted us so much. We did our homework and learned what the new VP's background was, the rise within his career, and our basic knowledge of what he would be stepping into. We knew what the role was, but our questions were focused on him/the new VP taking over. We wanted to know from him who he was, what blind spots we may have missed, and what blind spots he may have encountered. That session was all about us using the 3Ds of Success: Define, Develop, and Deliver. By the time the meeting ended, we had *defined* what he personally needed to be successful and how it aligned with the organization. He bought in and was happy to have a strong AMT to partner with. We *developed* an Action Plan based on his priorities and initiatives and jumped into *deliver* mode. He was excited and understood exactly how we had earned the trust of the organization.

Building Relationships Summary: 3 Things – 3 Steps

3 Things:

1. Know the Role
2. Know the Person
3. Know the Result

3 Steps:

1. Knowing the role comes from doing research. Gain an understanding of what someone in the type of position/level of the organization must do to be successful. What are the typical challenges, quantifiable metrics, and results they are required to deliver?

2. Getting to know the person will happen over time. Once you have proven yourself to be trustworthy, you can peel back more layers. Remember, it is about Trust, Value, and Teamwork.

3. When you *Define* the results that help the person in the role achieve success, you can then *Develop* a plan to get there, and by working with them as a team, they will see the value you *Deliver,* and your relationship will blossom.

Chapter 3: Expanding Relationships

Account Management Lifecycle

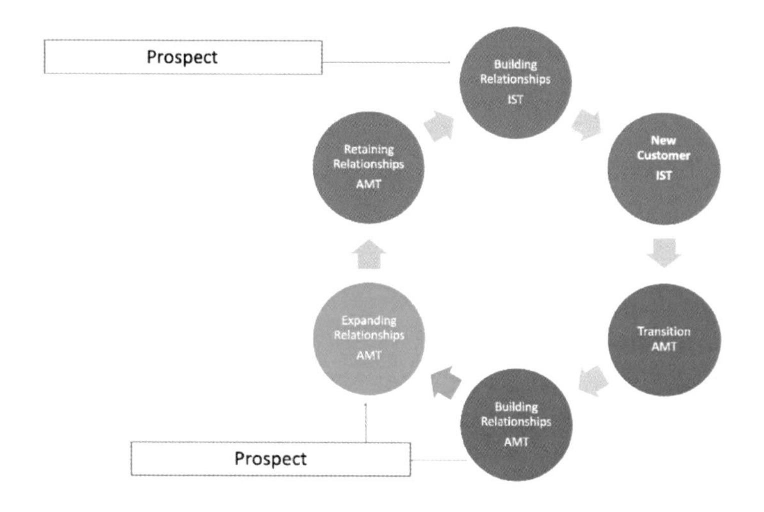

At some point, you must expand to other business units within the accounts you manage. This keeps you in good favor with sales leadership... Smile... Customers expand their business relationships because they consistently receive excellent service, quality, reliable products/services, competitive pricing, innovation, flexibility, and proactive communication. So where, when, and how do you start? I like to start during the Transition meeting. It is a good time because you have just set the cadence for communication.

The AMT should always be identifying areas to help their customers grow. The ability to collaborate with the customer based on their individual needs and shared vision of what success looks and feels like is priceless. This discovery can be done during Annual Strategy Meetings (ASM), Quarterly Business Reviews (QBR), Monthly Meetings (MM), and one-on-one Champion meetings. I say it's priceless because the cost of expanding to more users/stakeholders will come up in most conversations. You will increase your chances of expanding during these conversations by clearly mapping their OPIs to pain points, challenges, and projects. Then, showing ROI via success stories and measurable results how your products/services have and are helping other business units and companies like theirs.

Leveraging Internal Partners:

The more you know, the more you grow. This is where I encourage AMTs to differentiate themselves from the competition. Move beyond just being an expert on your products/services. Analyze what is going on in the customer's industry, the effects the economy is having on them, and insights you can offer that align with their OPIs. Lean into internal relationships with the Product and Customer-Based Marketing teams.

Have the SS work with the PT to identify upcoming and new features/functions in the product roadmap the customer can take advantage of. Then, collectively partner with the CBM team to assist with use cases and messaging. This is a window for the CBM team to send a "did you know" type of message or some marketing campaign via their preferred channel of communication to educate the customer. It also helps the AMT, so the customer does not feel they are always trying to sell them something. The AMT can support the messaging during the MMs with the intent to educate, not upsell or cross-sell.

Maximizing Your Meetings: The goal is for your customers to feel valued during each interaction and for all parties to get the most out of the time being spent together. Make sure the AMT interactions are focused on building and maintaining successful relationships. At the same time, positioning information that drives them to achieve their OPIs faster. With that said, since you developed the Action Plan during the ASM, use your MMs as sprints where everyone is focused on delivering/executing the actions agreed upon in the plan between each QBR.

Then leverage QBRs not only as check points and adjustment meetings but also as selling periods where upgrades and solutions that are a better fit can be presented and demoed. This process creates a duplicatable cadence and keeps everyone in alignment as a team driving toward desired results.

Getting through the noise: It is also important to realize your customers are busy. They have so much to do that many get buried in the day-to-day. You may have lots of valuable data to help them, but if they do not have time to consume and know how to leverage it to drive results, they will become frustrated. Imagine being your customer when it comes to receiving solicited and unsolicited information. Most websites claim an average person working in a corporate setting receives 120 emails per day and sends around 40 emails per day. This includes product promotions, newsletters and subscriptions, and communication with peers.

Now layer in the information they have asked you personally for and any new information the Marketing and Product teams share through email and other channels. At some point, it all blends together and becomes noise. That additional noise can make it hard for you to get the priority-based information through. Those times between MMs, if you have information you deem valuable, I recommend alerting them in advance. Depending on your relationship, send them a text message or call them so they know the message is coming through. Then, **BOLD** what is most important in your email. Send the highlights in bullet points so they can be quickly consumed. Point out *What* and *Why* it is valuable, followed by the *benefit* to them. When your customer has time, they can go back for the depth, but they know exactly what they are getting and how to leverage it. Then, during the MM or QBR, you can revisit the information and how you see it impacting their OPIs.

Customer-Centric: I quickly recognize when business units/teams work together. There is little duplication of questions and messages to the customer. These organizations operate in concert. They communicate internally before contacting the customer. This method of teamwork reduces chaos, confusion, stepping on toes, and frustrating the customer.

I believe another role of the AMT is a customer guardian, to shield the customer from becoming overwhelmed with too much noise from other parts of the company. In a perfect world, the AMT, PT, PMT, and CBM teams would have visibility into each account via a CRM or centralized tool that points out customer OPIs and the status of the account; is it good or bad? Most people are receptive to listening and openly share when things are going well. If the account is in good standing, it will set off triggers with targeted messages and storytelling that resonate with the customer via automation. If not in good standing, the messages would not go out. THAT would be big on helping to increase expansion opportunities.

White Space: One method of expanding is to identify white space within your accounts. White space refers to untapped or underserved opportunities. It represents the gap between the products/services currently offered by your company and the additional needs or desires of your customers that are not being addressed. Identifying white space involves understanding customer preferences, pain points, and unmet needs, as well as recognizing areas where competitors may be falling short. This comes back to *Trust*, *Value*, and *Teamwork*. I spoke about this in the building relationships chapter. As you begin to expand, you see the importance of having done so. It is you using PEEL and 3Ds during your ASM, QBRs, and MMs.

Upsell & Cross-sell Strategies:

Upselling involves educating your customer that the upgraded option may be more expensive, but it will provide ROI because it offers additional features, benefits, and value that align with their OPIs.

Cross-selling refers to offering complementary or related products/services to customers based on their current purchases or interests. The aim is to encourage customers to buy additional items that complement their original purchase or address related needs. The value of expanding within their existing business unit or other is by adding more of your company's products/services so they achieve their OPIs faster because access to resources significantly increases their ability to drive growth and revenues.

Show Value Delivered: As your AMT identifies these expansion opportunities, realize you must always prove value. The best way to do this is by using their words, and the numbers they have said provide value and ROI. Then, showcase these measurable results to your prospect via storytelling customer use cases that match their projects, challenges, and OPIs. Ask your champion to share their success with the other business unit within the same account. There is nothing like an internal success story that has/is helping achieve OPIs. Leverage the access to Power/C-Level executives you have built during ASMs or QBRs. This access to the people who can say yes or no and sign agreements is where you need to be to get deals done.

This method, in addition to mapping the capabilities of your product/services to their personal needs, is key. During your proposal, align measurable results, ROI, timelines, and how your

AMT will partner with them to execute the Action Plan. When packaged properly, the details will help the prospect gain budget approval and give you the opportunity to expand. You will most likely need to engage your Finance and Legal internal partners to make sure your pricing and approvals align with your company. Keep those relationships and your business cases strong, so those communications are a non-event. The sales process never stops. You will always find yourself using the PEEL method, being an A.C.E, and leveraging 3Ds.

Get high and stay high: When you partner with C-Level executives, you are high enough in the organization to get things done efficiently and effectively. Authority, accountability, strategic vision, resource allocation, cross-functional collaboration, faster decision-making, influence, negotiation, and opportunity for innovation are some of the advantages that decision-makers have at the C-Suite level. If you do not have it, do your best to gain access during your ASM and keep it.

Good vs. Bad

Good: When the AMT knows the intricacies of the customer's business due to consistent communication during the ASM, QBRs, and MMs, it keeps everyone aligned with their OPIs. It is also important for the AMT to be experts on their products/services so they can make suggestions and provide solutions to help their customers grow. As mentioned earlier in the chapter, leaning into internal relationships with PT, CBM, and others can be key to getting things done and sometimes shielding customers from extra noise. It takes everyone to achieve a customer-centric environment, which leads to upsell and cross-sell opportunities.

Bad: When the AMT is not an expert in their product/service, they do not collaborate with internal partners, and they are not running consistent ASM, QBRs, and MMs. This all leads to poor communication and lost opportunities to expand.

Personal Experience:

I have been fortunate to work with some good people throughout my sales career. They have been peers, partners, and customers. Most of the relationships have been solid, with good teamwork all around. As we know, there is no such thing as perfect. There have also been relationships that could not be repaired. I recall one customer where my AMT built a great relationship with two key individuals within the organization. One of them was a Chief Technology Officer (CTO), decision maker, and signer on a significant contract. The other was the Director of Information Technology (IT). They were both sincere and straight forward in their approach to doing business and the expectations of how our product/services should perform based on our company's documented Service Level Agreements (SLAs).

The account was transitioned to our AMT with a completed ATF and introductory meeting. We hit it off fast. Our personalities meshed well. During the introductory meeting, they both shared how they liked the product/service, but it did not always hold up to our SLAs. I quickly jumped into A.C.E mode so they knew I was listening to their concerns. Their response and appreciation were genuine. Their contract had 18 months remaining, and they pointed out they were open to renewing it with us and possibly expanding to more locations if we could work through a couple of SLA challenges. They were in a hyper-growth mode, and our products/services could really help them. The pushback they had was from their Chief Financial Officer (CFO). The reason was how our products/services impacted their ability to communicate with their customers and how their customers communicated with their

Sales and Customer Support teams. If we went down, the financial impact was significant.

Actions Taken: I coordinated an all-hands meeting where I pulled in our VPs in Customer Support, Customer Success, Sales, and my AMT core partners. We invited the customer's CTO, Dir of IT, and CFO. We followed the 3Ds of Success framework by *Defining* the challenges, what they needed to see to show improvement, a timeframe to achieve it, and how to earn their trust in us as a team and, more importantly, our product/service.

Our leadership was able to commit to a patch that would be implemented to temporarily solve the challenges to meet their expectations and our SLAs while they worked on a permanent solution. I collaborated with my CSM to *Develop* an Action Plan, which outlined each step of our approach. We did not leave anything to chance. We met twice per month for the first two months with a reduced group on both sides until everyone felt comfortable.

We then shifted to quarterly meetings after a 90-day period. The plan was working. We had shown our ability to *deliver* the results they needed. At that point, we had earned their trust. Over the following 6 months, we expanded locations and users, which equated to more than doubling their spending. At that moment, we were all happy because we were *delighting our customer*, which led to expansion.

Challenge: We were 12 months into our new relationship with 6 months to go in the contract and were negotiating an early renewal with incentives for a 3-year agreement and built-in expansion. We had been continuously communicating with the Development team on their progress in finding a permanent solution. They had not, and the patch was still in place. We were not excited about that but assured the customer we would find a permanent solution as we entered into this new contract agreement. With 5 months to go, the bottom began to fall out. The development team had not found a permanent solution to the previous challenges where the patch had been implemented. The patch started to fail, and the outages began again. The talks turned from happiness to frustration to what is now. We followed the same steps as we did before. This time around, we knew we just had to deliver in a short period of time. This time, the outage was deemed catastrophic based on the number of days they were down. We were well outside of our SLAs. Our leadership did not have a good response, so they followed the standard response in the SLA language, which leaned toward our company versus the customer. That template response did not go over well.

Actions Taken: Our AMT implemented 3Ds of Success. Part of our strategy this time around was to meet on a weekly basis with the CTO, VP of IT, and the CFO, who sat in once per month to basically tell us about their disappointment. We knew they had been vetting other companies, and after 45 days, they began migrating services to our competitor. It was a frustrating time because the AMT had worked so hard to build and expand on the personal and business relationship. We eventually lost that customer due to no fault of our own but product/service failure. I tell you this story because that is the reality of working with customers. You win some, you lose some. The goal is to win many, lose a few, and learn from the mistakes, so it does not happen as often. The challenges and lessons learned created a deeper bond between the AMT and the rest of the organization. We lost the customer but created a duplicatable roadmap by leveraging the 3Ds and having a *delighting the customer* mindset. It led to increased credibility throughout our organization and became the blueprint for how to build and expand relationships.

Expanding Relationships Summary: 3 Things – 3 Steps

3 Things:

1. Know your customer's business.

2. Get High and Stay High.

3. Leverage Your Internal Partners

3 Steps:

1. Knowing your customer's business is essential for building strong relationships, offering personalized solutions, identifying growth opportunities, and anticipating challenges. It can also help you differentiate yourself from your competitors and position your business for long-term success.

2. Working with decision-makers can provide significant value for your business or organization, including faster decision-making, clear communication, strategic alignment, stronger relationships, and greater influence. Decision makers have the authority to make important decisions quickly. Working directly with them can help you avoid delays and ensure that your proposals are considered and acted upon promptly.

3. Winning is a team sport. Leaning into your internal relationships/partners can differentiate you from the competition. Overall, teamwork in customer-centric roles enables organizations to provide a more comprehensive, efficient, and customer-focused experience. By leveraging the strengths of each team member and promoting

collaboration, you can enhance customer satisfaction and loyalty and ultimately achieve their OPIs.

Chapter 4: Retaining Relationships

Account Management Lifecycle

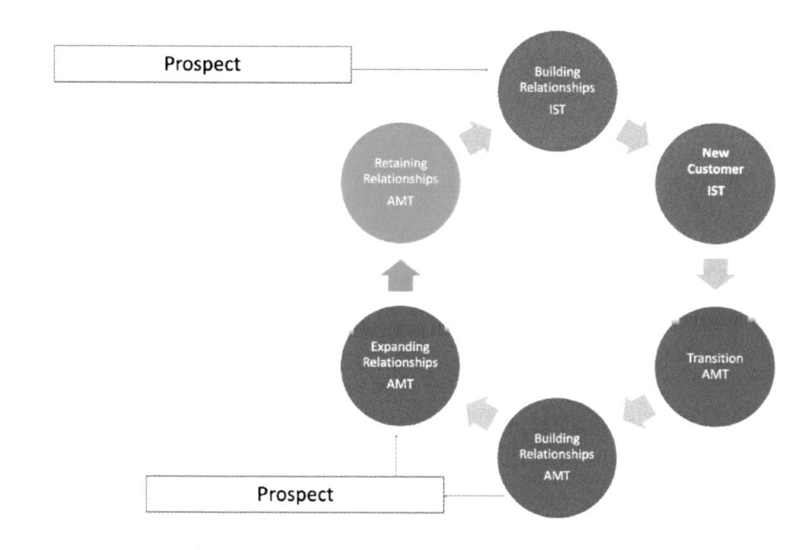

Customer retention refers to the ability of a business to retain its existing customers over a period of time. The process is ongoing and a critical aspect of a company's overall growth and profitability strategy. It comes back to *delighting the customer.*

A study by TARP Research as far back as 1999 uncovered the fact that for every 26 unhappy customers, only 1 will bother to make a formal complaint. The rest will either stay where they are disappointed or will silently take their business elsewhere. An even worse situation is when an unhappy customer begins to speak negatively about your company via multiple media channels instead of complaining to you and your company about their experience. The White House Office of Consumer Affairs found that a dissatisfied customer will tell between 9-15 people. About 13% tell more than 20 people, which leads to damage to reputation, loss of potential customers and revenue.

You can retain customers by consistently providing outstanding experiences, actively engaging with them, and continuously improving. Your ability to continuously build strong relationships through trust, value, and teamwork creates loyalty and encourages repeat business.

The Value of Customer Retention:

- Revenue Stability: Retaining existing customers helps stabilize a company's revenue stream. Happy/delighted customers become loyal customers and are more likely to continue purchasing from a business. This provides a consistent and predictable source of revenue. This stability can help mitigate the impact of fluctuating market conditions or customer acquisition challenges.

- Cost Efficiency: Acquiring new customers typically requires more resources and investment compared to retaining existing ones. The cost of marketing, advertising, and sales efforts to attract new customers can be significantly higher than maintaining relationships with current customers. Therefore, customer retention can lead to cost savings and improved profitability.

- Customer Lifetime Value (CLV): Customer retention is closely linked to the concept of Customer Lifetime Value, which refers to the total value a customer brings to a business over the entire duration of their relationship. Loyal customers tend to have higher CLV as they continue to make repeat purchases, refer others, and potentially upgrade to higher-priced products or services.

- Positive Word-of-Mouth and Referrals: Satisfied and loyal customers often become advocates for a business. They are more likely to recommend the company to friends, family, or colleagues, leading to valuable word-of-mouth marketing and referral opportunities. These referrals can generate new customers at a lower cost and with a higher likelihood of conversion.

- Competitive Advantage: Building strong customer relationships and fostering loyalty can create a competitive advantage. A business with high customer retention rates can differentiate itself from competitors by providing superior customer service, personalized experiences, and a deeper understanding of its customer's needs and preferences. This differentiation can help attract and retain more customers over time.

- Feedback and Insights: Long-term customer relationships provide opportunities for businesses to gather valuable feedback and insights. Engaged customers are more likely to provide feedback on products/services and overall experiences, enabling the company to make informed decisions and improvements. This feedback loop can enhance product development, customer service, and overall business operations.

As you can see, customer retention is significant. It contributes to revenue stability, cost efficiency, higher customer lifetime value, positive word-of-mouth, competitive advantage, and access to valuable customer insights. By prioritizing customer retention strategies, businesses can foster loyalty, drive sustainable growth, and increase profitability in the long run.

The Keys to Retention: The keys lie within the actions we have been talking about. They are the building blocks to delighting the customer. You build trust, value, and teamwork via consistent communication, encouraging customer engagement via ASMs, QBRs, and MMs. At each step, you are using PEEL, the 3Ds, and teaming with your internal partners, so your messaging is timely, and your product/service is delivering results to help them achieve their OPIs.

An article written by Mailchimp points out that 89% of customers are more likely to complete an additional purchase following a good customer service experience. According to Zippia, "The average customer retention rate is 75.5% across all industries. The media and the professional service industries both have the highest worldwide customer retention rates at 84% each. The hospitality, travel, and restaurant industry have the lowest customer retention rate at 55%, followed by retail at 63%." Article written Jan 16, 2023. If you can retain 85% - 90% of your customers/contract value, you are in a good position for long-term success.

Maximizing Product Team & Marketing Partners (Product Marketing & Customer Based Marketing): These two teams are vital when thinking of the customer experience. The Product team's ability to understand the customer journey is key when it comes to creating the roadmap. They must know during the product lifecycle what, when, and how the product/service impacts the customer so it can be communicated properly to the PMT. This allows them to build the go-to-market strategy and align product values to messaging, which enables the CBM team to deliver timely messaging to the customer base in tandem with the sales organization and AMT, all leading to an increase in customer retention.

I encourage the AMT to check in with the PT, PMT, and CBM internal partners whenever possible so they are all in alignment on what is and what is not working for the customers they work with. The Solution Specialist (SS) can also be instrumental in helping the AM and CSM connect the dots on product/service use cases.

Securing the Renewal: The same as with expanding, the AMT must show value delivered and capabilities based on future OPIs. How do you get there? As you enter the final year of your contract, position the renewal conversation during the ASM. *Define* the OPIs for the upcoming years you plan on securing a contract term. Then, *develop* an Action Plan that fits and begin *delivering* upon it. During your QBRs and MMs, continue to check the boxes to ensure you are on track. Position an incentive for those customers who are open to doing an early renewal. It helps lock in the relationship sooner than later and avoid any unforeseen challenges that may come up if you wait until the end. This can be done if you have demonstrated value throughout the relationship.

As mentioned during the introduction, it is prove it or lose it time. Use PEEL in combination with the 3Ds. Everyone from your champion and decision makers to the Finance team for your customer will scrutinize the value from the past, present, and future. Hold firm during your negotiations. As long as your proposal and plans align with helping them drive revenue and growth, you are in a good position. Then it comes down to what each side needs to make the numbers work for a win/win situation. Trust, value, and teamwork, in conjunction with achieving OPIs, get the deal done.

Good vs. Bad:

Good: When your customer gets what they paid for and enhanced features/functions during the term of their contract without additional costs. It shows your company is consistently working to deliver a better experience by executing its vision and roadmap. When the AMT and other internal partners are in constant communication via multiple channels and make needed adjustments to delight the customer based on their feedback, you are doing a good job. The more your customer trusts you, the more secure they will be to build their business strategy using your products/services. They will do so because you have proven to deliver what is needed for them to drive revenue and growth. That is a good business relationship.

Bad: When the customer is not being delighted. Anytime the AMT and internal partners are not listening to the customer and making the needed adjustments to deliver what the customer is paying for, it puts the account at risk, and that is not good.

Personal Experience:

I recall working on a multimillion-dollar deal where the Champion/customer and I had agreed upon what we both thought was a solid framework that could be easily agreed on. We collaborated on what their leadership needed to see, and then I created my proposal. It clearly defined the challenges we helped them overcome, the measurable value that had been received, and the positive impact it had on the company's growth. In addition, I collaborated with my AMT members, internal partners, and the customer to develop an Action Plan with timelines and deliverables that would provide them with double-digit year-over-year growth during the term of the contract. My Champion and I were pleased and ready to present. We knew there would be some pushback from our respective Finance and Legal teams and were prepared to answer any questions that came up.

Challenge: The challenge we had was the timing of the negotiations. We found ourselves with delays on both sides that took weeks to overcome. The customer Finance team did not like the annual percentage increase. They wanted a lower percentage, and their Legal team wanted more favorable terms, which included some downturn clauses due to economic headwinds. In these situations, I like to pull together my success team and map out what comes first. "Chicken or the egg?" I basically mean, do we negotiate with the customer first and get their buy-in/best and final or our company's Finance and Legal? Either way, we would find ourselves at the same place needed to get a deal done with a couple of days left in the quarter. That is never a good feeling. You must love sales and this type of emotional roller coaster to make a career of it.

Actions Taken: I met with my champion to understand what their Finance and Legal bottom lines/best and final would be to get a deal done in a short period of time. We worked together and adjusted the proposal with solid talking points that created a win/win situation. Then, we outlined and agreed upon the actions we each would take with our collective teams.

My champion helped facilitate a meeting with their Finance and Legal. We set the meeting time. I then communicated the plan to my AMT leadership, and we presented it to our Finance and Legal teams to get their buy-in prior to the customer meeting. There was just as much posturing and selling to our internal team as it was to the customer. Ultimately, we came to an agreement that matched the best and final for the customer.

When both sides attended the meeting, we went through the formalities of introductions and our purpose for being there, thanked everyone for their time, and proceeded to discuss just the points we were hung up on. Because my Champion/customer and I had prepared with our own teams, we all came into the meeting ready to get a deal done. We made the needed compromises for a win/win situation and got the deal done in the final hour of the day. It was intense as we went back and forth to secure the contract and purchase order to book the deal, but we made it.

It was another example of consistent communication and collaboration. Our AMT had built trust with everyone needed to get a deal done. The lessons from this experience were to make sure the AMT and internal partners were aligned with the champion and all decision-makers on what they perceived as value. Then, for me/AM to clearly articulate the impact of past, present, and expected future results based on the customer's OPIs. Once that was done, we tied it all back to ROI. It made the term and price conversation much easier.

Retaining Relationships Summary

3 Things:

1. Sold relationship with your champion /customer.

2. Consistent communication and collaboration with the AMT, internal partners, and champion.

3. Be an A.C.E – Acknowledge, Confirm, and Execute what you say you will do.

3 Steps:

1. Spend extra time getting to know your champion/customer. They are people who want to be appreciated and respected, just like you. Help them look good, and they will do the same for you.

2. Conversations lead to collaboration. Make sure you know what the individual, their team, and company need to achieve their OPIs. Then, work with them and your internal partners to do what it takes to secure business. You are leveraging the trust you have built, the value you have delivered, and achieving success through teamwork.

3. During each conversation, be an A.C.E. Ask deeper level questions to really understand, *Acknowledge* what you hear, *Confirm* your understanding of what needs to be done so you get it correct, and then develop a plan you can *Execute*. Be vulnerable by letting your champion know your goal is to consistently partner with them to align the correct resources to their OPIs. Winning together as a team is what you are there to do.

Conclusion: Stay the Course

"Stay the course" is an expression that means to continue with a plan or course of action despite challenges, difficulties, or setbacks. It encourages perseverance, determination, and commitment to one's goals, even when faced with obstacles or doubts. This phrase is often used to motivate individuals or groups to maintain their resolve and not give up in the face of adversity. It implies that by staying focused and dedicated, one is more likely to achieve their desired outcome in the long run.

I point this out because no matter how long you have been in sales, you will have accounts, customers, and situations that are out of your control. There will be times when, no matter how much effort you put forth, how savvy and a good communicator you are, you will not be able to build, expand, or retain relationships. In these situations, implement PEEL and the 3Ds on yourself, and stay the course. Remain positive, keep your energy high, control your emotions, and seek advice from your success partners. Then make the adjustments needed so you can lead again. Always stick to the basics. Make sure you are checking all the boxes of what is required for you in your role. Internally, remain aligned with your leadership team on sales pipeline hygiene, completing your reports on time, and continuing to collaborate with your Internal Partners.

When checking all the boxes, it allows your advisors to see if there are gaps. If there are, they can provide resources, feedback, and encouragement to help get you back on course. If there are no gaps, their advice will help keep your confidence high. This leads to trust, value, and teamwork. Externally, continue building relationships, strategizing with your customers, and running your ASMs, QBRs, and MMs until the time is right. Use PEEL and the 3Ds to help *delight your customers* until you begin seeing results, and continue to stay the course.

Relationships are about communication. Your ability to partner with internal and external teams is important. It takes collaboration to build, expand, and retain relationships. Your AMT, along with the internal partners such as the Product Team, Product Marketing, Customer Marketing, Customer Service, and others, have significant roles when it comes to *Delighting the Customer*. When done in concert, it leads to Trust, Value, and Teamwork. This is why PEEL is so important. As previously stated, you always have *People* who have a certain level of *Energy* and *Emotion* depending on what they are dealing with. The same people have a need or desire to *Lead* themselves or be led through their challenges and blind spots to achieve whatever they deem is a success.

Your ability to leverage the PEEL method will help you go layers deeper in your communication while building stronger, more trusting relationships. And when you combine it with the 3Ds of Success framework, you increase your percentages of expanding and retaining those relationships.

If you do not already have it, I encourage you to adopt a *customer-first mindset*. Imagine how valuable your AMT will be to your company because you spend a good portion of your time learning who the people are you sell products/services to. That, along with just as deep an understanding of how their company works as you do your own. This level of depth will allow you to position what is needed for them to achieve their OPIs. This is my perfect world vision of Account Management. I realize nothing works all the time, but I do believe if done as outlined, your retention rates will jump from the average 75.5% industry-wide to 85% - 100%.

If you have found a few more layers of value in Onion Based-Relationships you can implement in your Account Management business that lead to building, expanding, and retaining relationships, then my purpose is fulfilled. Thank you for sharing this time and space with me. I would love to hear how you are leveraging the tools and ideas. Keep peeling back those layers, having consistent conversations, and growing.

John H. Brown

3Ds of Success Growth Plan- 2023 (Sample)

Define: Top 3 Goals This Year	Develop: 3 Actions/Goal	Develop: Why & Reward	Deliver: Success Team	Deliver: Expected Results/Q1	Deliver: Expected Results/Q2	Deliver: Expected Results/Q3	Deliver: Expected Results/Q4
1) President's Club	1) $300K New CV 2) 90% Retention 3) Expand Relationships	Why: • Recognition • Money Reward: Personal Satisfaction	• Leadership Support • CSM & SS Teamwork • Internal Partners	Renew: • Account 1 • Account 2	Renew: • Account 3 • Account 4	Renew: • Account 5 • Account 6	Expand Seats
2) $400K Earnings	1) Strong Engagement 2) 20% Expansion/Acct 3) $700K New CV	Why: • New Level • Building for Retirement Reward: TBD	• Leadership Support • CSM & SS Teamwork • Internal Partners	Expand Users: CV Growth- $150K	Expand Users: CV Growth- $150K	Expand Seats CV Growth- $100K	Expand Seats CV Growth- $300K
3) Leadership Advancement	1) Management Training Course 2) Join 2 Committees 3) Mentorship Role	Why: • Education • Exposure Reward: Growth	• Leadership Support • CSM & SS Teamwork • Internal Partners	Peer Mentor • TBD • TBD	• Active in Committees • Active in Mentorship	Management Training Participation	President's Club Achievement

Resources & Tools

3Ds of Success Growth Plan

Account Management Lifecycle (AML)

Account Review Process (ARP)

Account Transition Form (ATF)

https://browndevelopments.com/tools

Made in the USA
Las Vegas, NV
13 October 2023

79033636R00040